21st Century Skills Library

GLOBAL PERSPECTIVES

PANDEMICS

Robert Green

Cherry Lake Publishing
Ann Arbor, Michigan

Published in the United States of America by Cherry Lake Publishing
Ann Arbor, Michigan
www.cherrylakepublishing.com

Content Adviser: Scott P. Layne, MD, Professor of Epidemiology, Department of Public Health, University of California, Los Angeles

Photo Credits: Cover and page 1, © iStockphoto.com/Keithbrooks; page 4, © Danita Delimont/Alamy; page 6, © Holger Mette, used under license from Shutterstock, Inc.; page 7, © Steve Hamblin/Alamy; page 9, © Peter Treanor/Alamy; pages 10 and 25, © Terry Whittaker/Alamy; page 13, © iStockphoto.com/dra-schwartz; page 14, © EIGHTFISH/Alamy; page 16, © Iain Masterton/Alamy; page 18, © MedicalRF.com/Alamy; page 20, © Blend Images/Alamy; page 22, © AA World Travel Library/Alamy; page 23, © Vario Images GmbH & Co.KG/Alamy; page 26, © Laurence Gough, used under license from Shutterstock, Inc.

Map by XNR Productions Inc.

Library of Congress Cataloging-in-Publication Data
Green, Robert.
Pandemics / by Robert Green.
   p. cm.—(Global perspectives)
Includes index.
ISBN-13: 978-1-60279-129-9
ISBN-10: 1-60279-129-5
1. Epidemics—Juvenile literature. 2. Communicable diseases—Juvenile literature. I. Title. II. Series.
RA653.5.G73 2008
614.4—dc22   2007034370

Cherry Lake Publishing would like to acknowledge the work of
The Partnership for 21st Century Skills.
Please visit www.21stcenturyskills.org *for more information.*

TABLE OF CONTENTS

CHAPTER ONE

AN IDEAL GLOBAL CITIZEN

*People walk through a crowded terminal at Chicago's O'Hare
International Airport. Airplanes make it easy to travel around the world.*

Sakda Srichaphan stood at the window of a hotel convention center,
looking proudly over his home city of Bangkok, Thailand. The
golden-tipped Buddhist temples glinted in the powerful sun, and the

sluggish, muddy waters of the Chao Phraya River meandered by the hotel.

He was proud because he was to play host to students from all over the world, who had come to Thailand for the International Global Issues Summit. He greeted them, one after another, as they arrived at the convention center and joined him at the window to look over this Southeast Asian city.

"It's wonderful," said Asger Knudsen, a delegate from the northern European country of Denmark. "I have never been to Asia before. It makes me feel like a real world traveler to fly so far from home. But honestly, I can't believe how easy it was to get here. I flew directly from Copenhagen, the capital of Denmark, to Bangkok. It's amazing how air travel has made the world so much smaller."

At this, Sakda, conscious of his role in the summit, took the chance to introduce some very worrying aspects of global travel. "Do you know," he said, "that there is a global citizen even more suited to international travel?"

"Who is it?" asked Asger, thinking that he was a pretty good global traveler.

"This traveler knows no boundaries," said Sakda, making it sound more and more like a riddle. "He goes where he wishes, and he needs no

A Buddhist monk looks out over the city of Bangkok.

passport. He can travel on a plane without anyone knowing, and he is very hard to stop."

Asger made a face. He couldn't focus on coming up with an answer. He was still a little distracted after the long flight and the bustle of Bangkok, with its pedicabs, river traffic, and Buddhist monks in colorful robes. "So, who is he?" he asked with great curiosity.

"'He' is a disease," said Sakda, smiling gently. "He is more ideally suited to global life than any of us. And the more humans travel, the more chances he has to travel along with us, infecting people all over the world."

Sakda's story had a lot of truth to it, and it got Asger and the other students around them thinking about the reason

Many diseases spread easily in crowded conditions.

they had come to the global summit. For a week, they would be discussing the dangers of pandemics—diseases that spread quickly from person to person, until they affect an entire region or even spread all the way around the globe.

The students gathered for the summit in an Asian capital, because two of the most recent scares of pandemic disease cropped up in that area. In 2002 and 2003, the world was alarmed by an outbreak of SARS, or Severe Acute Respiratory Syndrome, a deadly respiratory disease. It spread from China to other places around the globe, mostly by infected air travelers. In 2004, a form of influenza known as avian influenza, or bird flu, was detected in Vietnam and sparked renewed fears of a pandemic.

The students had already become familiar with one another by communicating through e-mail. They had sent each other reports on pandemics and different diseases, and told each other about the health scares in their own countries. Over the next week, they would try to develop a better understanding of the frightening possibilities of pandemic outbreaks. They would also look at what people around the world are doing to prevent this global danger.

CHAPTER TWO

What the Birds Tell Us

Many people in Hong Kong and other affected cities wore face masks during the SARS outbreak.

As the delegates to the summit got down to the business of discussing pandemics, Asger was still thinking about what a pandemic was. "If a pandemic is a disease that affects a lot of people, then why are cancer and diabetes not considered pandemics?" he asked. "And what is the difference between a pandemic and an epidemic?" Other students agreed that these were logical questions.

"I think I can answer your questions," said Marie Pepin, a young delegate from Canada who had been studying the issue for weeks before the summit. An epidemic is an outbreak of a disease that affects a lot of people in a particular region. A pandemic affects even more people, over a much larger area, or even around the world. "A pandemic is caused by a new disease that we are unprepared for," she said. "It is also one that spreads easily when people come into contact with other people. That is why cancer is not a pandemic, even though it affects people all over the world."

⁌ ⁌ ⁌

One of the reasons that pandemics are a global problem is that no one can predict exactly when and where a pandemic will break out or how many people it will infect. Another reason pandemics pose such a serious threat is the fact that the organisms that cause diseases can **mutate**, or change. This ability to mutate makes them unpredictable.

Influenza, more commonly known as the flu, is a good example. It is a virus that is passed from human to human by close contact. Common strains of the flu, which can be passed by sneezing or drinking out of the same glass as someone infected, crop up every year all over the world. The virus is highly **contagious**, meaning it can be easily passed from one person to another.

People buy and sell live chickens and ducks at a poultry market in Vietnam. Avian flu can be spread by close contact with chickens and other birds.

Other kinds of influenza are present in animals, including birds. In 2004, people in the Southeast Asian nation of Vietnam began to get sick, and some died. Doctors determined that they had contracted avian flu, a kind of influenza common in birds. These people got the flu from being in close contact with chickens and other types of birds. The disease had jumped from birds to humans, greatly worrying doctors and

Learning & Innovation Skills

Epidemiologists are scientists who study diseases. When a new disease breaks out, these scientists act like detectives. They track infected patients to understand how the disease is spreading. They also look closely at the disease by doing laboratory experiments to identify the disease. Finally, they try to find a cure for the disease. These medical detectives are very important to global efforts to stop pandemics.

If epidemiology sounds like a career you might be interested in, make sure you take as many science and math classes as you can. Work to develop your critical thinking skills, too. You'll need them to figure out the connections between people who come down with a disease and to try to come up with ways to stop the disease's spread.

epidemiologists, people who study epidemics. Some of these people died from the bird flu, while others recovered after a period of sickness.

Because avian flu is common in birds but does not usually infect humans, many scientists believed that the disease had mutated. The mutation created a stronger virus that could more easily be passed to humans, making it more dangerous. Thinking that the disease would spread all over the world, many people predicted a pandemic. For a pandemic to occur, a disease must be strong enough to jump easily from one person to another, infecting many people quickly. As it turned out, this new strain of avian flu did not pass between people as easily as scientists had feared.

The avian flu outbreak in Vietnam was contained, or stopped, by isolating the people infected by the disease. Keeping them away from other people made sure that they would not pass it on. But epidemiologists still fear that the disease could mutate again and become even more deadly to human beings. Today, governments all over the world are studying the disease and trying to prevent an avian flu pandemic.

✢ ✢ ✢

"So was the bird flu a pandemic?" asked Asger, a little worried that he had entirely missed a pandemic in his own generation without even knowing it.

"No," said Marie, "because it did not spread as quickly as people had predicted. It did not spread easily from one person to another. But it could have been a pandemic if the virus had been more **virulent**, or stronger. We were very lucky!"

Scientists are working to develop a vaccine for avian flu.

CHAPTER THREE

A Close Call

*Travelers at a railway station in Guangdong, China, wear
masks to protect themselves from the SARS virus.*

"We had a very similar scare with a type of respiratory disease
known as Severe Acute Respiratory Syndrome, or SARS," said Sakda. "In
Thailand, we were very worried, and many people wore masks to prevent
being infected."

"Was SARS a pandemic?" asked Asger, still trying to get a good idea of what made a pandemic.

"It was very close. Some people say it was a pandemic, but others say it wasn't," said Sakda. "The disease spread rapidly and infected many people. In the end, quick measures such as wearing masks and isolating infected people contained the spread of SARS. One lasting effect is that people all over the world have become much more concerned with reacting quickly to diseases that could blossom into pandemics."

⁜ ⁜ ⁜

SARS first appeared in China's Guangdong Province. No one knows for sure how the first victim got the disease, but a viral mutation is suspected. Within a few days of being infected with SARS, patients begin to show signs of serious illness. Unlike avian flu, it can spread easily from person to person.

SARS spread quickly to other people in China. It also spread to Hong Kong, which has a busy international airport. From there, it traveled to Taiwan and other Asian countries and to Europe and Canada. People feared that SARS would end up causing a global health crisis.

One particularly worrisome feature of the outbreak was the spread of SARS in hospitals. Since doctors were not sure exactly how to treat SARS, the disease spread to other people when SARS patients checked in to hospitals. SARS requires the isolation of a patient in a special room

A traveler is checked for symptoms of SARS at a bus station in China.

that prevents the disease from spreading. This illustrates the difficulties of treating unfamiliar diseases.

The rapid spread of SARS, especially through infected people flying on airplanes, highlights the need for global cooperation when a new disease breaks out. One very troubling event in the SARS story was China's reaction to the initial outbreak. Chinese doctors and government officials feared that knowledge of the outbreak would cause a panic, so they tried to keep it hidden and did not report many cases of SARS.

While the Chinese fear of public unrest is understandable, an outbreak of a highly contagious disease like SARS requires a quick response. That is the only way to prevent an outbreak from becoming a pandemic. Other countries must be warned, and international efforts must be made to control the outbreak. The Chinese government received much criticism for its handling of the SARS outbreak. Chinese leaders have vowed to be more open in the future.

The World Health Organization (WHO), established by the United Nations, monitors for signs of an outbreak of a contagious disease. This international health organization also helps coordinate responses to an outbreak. Once SARS was identified, international cooperation happened quickly. All over the world, people were screened at airports for signs of the disease, and patients were isolated so that they did not infect more people. The efforts proved successful, but it was a very close call.

21st Century Content

To govern effectively, leaders must balance many different concerns. When Chinese leaders resisted talking openly about the outbreak of SARS, they were trying to prevent panic and the problems that could result from the panic. But the disease was stopped much faster after more information was provided. The Chinese government got the balance wrong in that case. But all governments must make similarly tough decisions. When a new disease appears, citizens may criticize leaders for not being prepared for a pandemic outbreak. But when there is no threat of disease, they may complain that the government should spend the country's money on more immediate concerns. Decision making becomes a difficult balance when leaders are faced with these often conflicting concerns.

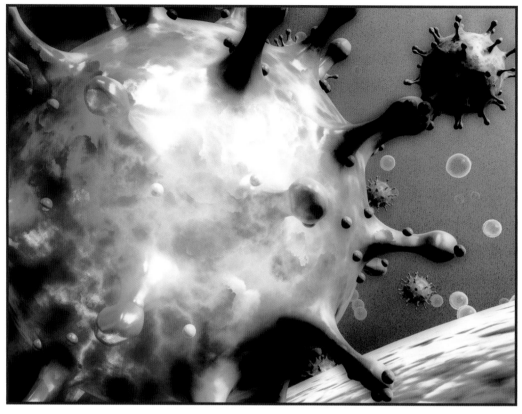

A powerful microscope is needed to see the SARS virus.

Government leaders all over the world understand the importance of preventing pandemics. They have increased their cooperation with other nations to help prevent and limit outbreaks of infectious diseases. This is very important because a pandemic can be devastating. To see just how serious a pandemic can be to the nations of the world, we need only look to the past.

CHAPTER FOUR

LESSONS FROM HISTORY

"So if the SARS outbreak was contained and didn't result in the global disaster that some had predicted, what is a real pandemic and why are people so worried about them?" asked Asger.

At this point, Anne Haskell, from the state of Kansas in the United States, rose to address the summit. She had been waiting for her chance to tell the delegates about a pandemic that broke out in her state in 1918.

"In Kansas, soldiers at Fort Riley, an army base, were becoming very sick," she said. "Doctors were uncertain what the disease was, and within a short time the disease began to spread around the world. It spread as far as the Arctic and to remote island groups. This disease truly knew no borders."

✢ ✢ ✢

The outbreak of the flu strain known as Spanish influenza raced around the globe from 1918 to 1919. It is estimated to have killed up to 5 percent of the entire world's population. In the United States, more than 500,000 people died.

This strain of influenza was transmitted from pigs. One of the most surprising features of the disease was that it killed so many young healthy people. Most diseases are especially hard on children and the elderly,

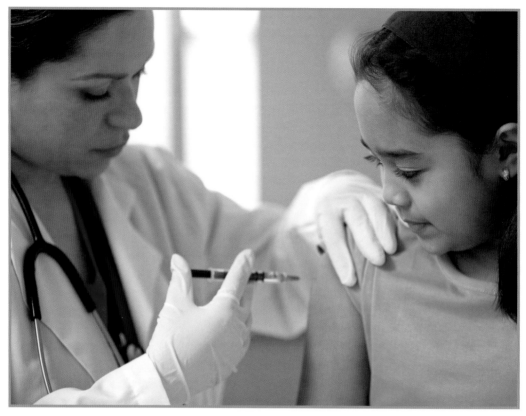

Vaccines help prevent many diseases.

whose bodies do not fight diseases as well. The Spanish flu, however, thrived in the communities of soldiers who had been fighting in World War I (1914–1918). The men lived in close quarters and infected each other. Troop ships carried the disease from place to place.

Hospitals were overrun with patients. Trains and ships became dangerous places, and many businesses had a hard time running because so many people were sick. People tried to go about their daily lives wearing masks, but death was everywhere. In addition to the health problems, the Spanish flu pandemic caused enormous problems for the world economy.

A true pandemic like the Spanish flu outbreak of 1918–1919 affects everything. People become sick and die, and the functioning of a country is threatened by the size of the disaster. This can cause hardship even for people who are not sick.

As SARS was spreading in the Far East in 2003, tourists and businesspeople started to travel less. Airlines and hotels lost money, and many other businesses suffered as a result. The disease had a ripple effect in the economy—its damage slowly

Learning & Innovation Skills

When new diseases break out, drug companies try to come up with vaccines to prevent them or medicines to help people get better after they have been infected. Companies that make medicines do so to make a profit. When a new drug comes out, the price is usually very high. The company includes the cost of doing the research to come up with the new medicine in the price. This often makes new drugs too expensive for some people to buy, especially in poor countries. To solve the problem, some government leaders and other activists try to convince drug companies to provide medicines to people in poor countries at a price that is lower than what they sell it for in the United States, Canada, and other richer countries. This way poor patients can get the medicine, and the drug company can still profit from its invention.

If you owned a drug company, what would you do? Would you agree to sell your medicines for a lower price in poor countries? Why or why not?

Derry Public Library

Many hotels lost money during the SARS outbreak.

spread, until it affected many people. Because so many businesses cross international borders, the economic effects were felt nearly everywhere.

❖ ❖ ❖

"So even if you don't get sick during the outbreak of a pandemic, you can suffer in other ways," said Asger.

"Exactly," said Anne. "We can all be affected by a health crisis because the countries of the world are tied together in so many ways."

CHAPTER FIVE

GLOBAL MONITORING

*Scientists around the world are reseaching avian flu
and other diseases that may cause pandemics.*

"If the outbreak of a disease from around the world can be carried into our own countries in a matter of hours or days, what can we do to protect ourselves?" asked Asger. "It seems that the problem is just a little too big for anyone or even any country to handle."

The SARS outbreak was linked to human contact with palm civits.

"That's true," said Sakda. "That is why doctors and health professionals all over the world cooperate with each other. In fact, there are monitors, people who watch for signs of disease outbreaks, to help prevent them from spreading."

❖ ❖ ❖

The SARS outbreak in China was picked up by people monitoring local news reports for health information. Even though China played down the threat at first, news still got out. Once it did, health agencies all over the world sprang into action.

Aside from coordinating global efforts to fight disease, one of the World Health Organization's main functions is to gather information from medical groups in different countries and share it with others. When SARS broke out, the WHO sent experts to help determine where the disease came from. They reported these findings to other members of the group to help stop SARS from spreading.

SARS, for example, was linked to animals known as palm civets, which were being handled by humans in southern China. SARS appeared to have come from contact with these fruit-eating mammals. This information has helped countries

One factor that slowed the response to the SARS outbreak in China was the slowness of the translation of local reports of sick people from Chinese to other languages. Information is only useful if we can understand it. And to understand it, it must be translated into a language that we understand. Organizations like the World Health Organization regularly translate information into different languages to assist in spreading information quickly.

Learning other languages is just one way to build a bridge between cultures. What are some other ways to develop a better understanding of people from other countries?

Computers make it easier for researchers to record and share data.

around the globe handle animals in a safer manner and check them for diseases potentially dangerous to humans.

Scientists today are working on vaccines for these diseases. Vaccines could prevent an outbreak by preparing our bodies to fight the diseases even before they arrive. All of this, however, will take a lot of research that will involve people in many countries.

✥ ✥ ✥

"So even though pandemics can ride with us on planes and ignore national boundaries, we can fight them by sharing information even more rapidly than a plane can travel," said Sakda.

He was proud that the summit had been so successful. The student delegates had faced the dangers of pandemics, shared ideas, and learned what could be done to prevent pandemics in the future.

"In other words," said Asger, "meetings like this one bring us closer to a common understanding of pandemics."

"Exactly," said Sakda as he shook Asger's hand and said good-bye to all the delegates. "And we must keep in contact with each other so that we can continue to share information."

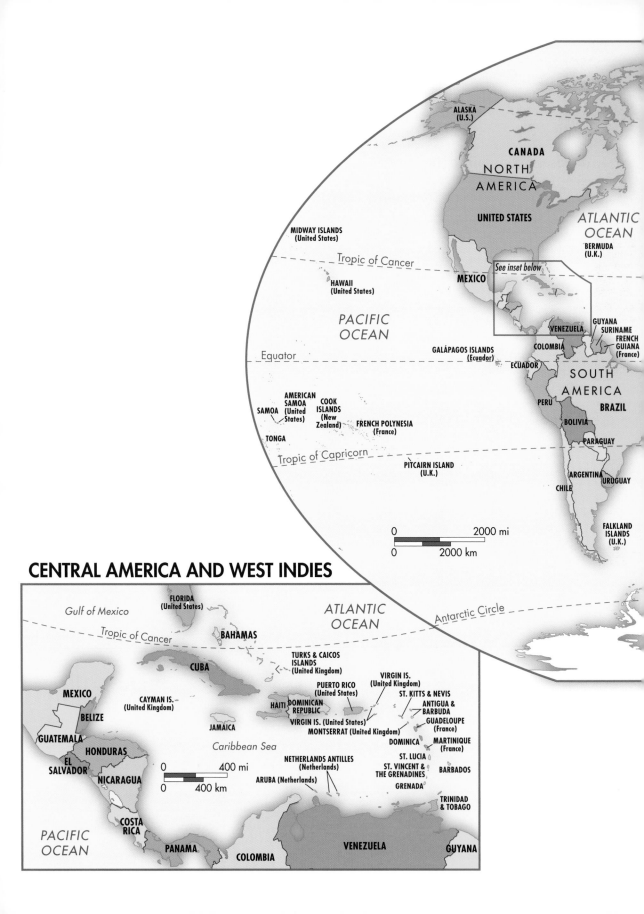

ALASKA
(U.S.)

CANADA

NORTH
AMERICA

UNITED STATES

ATLANTIC
OCEAN

MIDWAY ISLANDS
(United States)

BERMUDA
(U.K.)

Tropic of Cancer

See inset below

MEXICO

HAWAII
(United States)

PACIFIC
OCEAN

GALÁPAGOS ISLANDS
(Ecuador)

VENEZUELA

GUYANA
SURINAME
FRENCH
GUIANA
(France)

COLOMBIA

ECUADOR

Equator

SOUTH
AMERICA

AMERICAN
SAMOA
(United
States)

COOK
ISLANDS
(New
Zealand)

PERU

BRAZIL

SAMOA

FRENCH POLYNESIA
(France)

BOLIVIA

TONGA

PARAGUAY

Tropic of Capricorn

PITCAIRN ISLAND
(U.K.)

ARGENTINA

URUGUAY

CHILE

0   2000 mi

0   2000 km

FALKLAND
ISLANDS
(U.K.)

CENTRAL AMERICA AND WEST INDIES

FLORIDA
(United States)

ATLANTIC
OCEAN

Antarctic Circle

Gulf of Mexico

Tropic of Cancer

BAHAMAS

TURKS & CAICOS
ISLANDS
(United Kingdom)

CUBA

VIRGIN IS.
(United Kingdom)

MEXICO

CAYMAN IS.
(United Kingdom)

PUERTO RICO
(United States)

ST. KITTS & NEVIS

BELIZE

HAITI
DOMINICAN
REPUBLIC

ANTIGUA &
BARBUDA

JAMAICA

GUADELOUPE
(France)

GUATEMALA

VIRGIN IS. (United States)
MONTSERRAT (United Kingdom)

MARTINIQUE
(France)

HONDURAS

Caribbean Sea

DOMINICA

EL
SALVADOR

ST. LUCIA

NICARAGUA

0   400 mi

NETHERLANDS ANTILLES
(Netherlands)

ST. VINCENT &
THE GRENADINES

BARBADOS

0   400 km

ARUBA (Netherlands)

GRENADA

COSTA
RICA

TRINIDAD
& TOBAGO

PACIFIC
OCEAN

PANAMA

COLOMBIA

VENEZUELA

GUYANA

ARCTIC OCEAN

GREENLAND
(Denmark)

SVALBARD
(Norway)

Arctic Circle

ICELAND

RUSSIA

ASIA

EUROPE

KAZAKHSTAN

MONGOLIA

GEORGIA

UZBEKISTAN

KYRGYZSTAN

AZORES
(Portugal)

ARMENIA
TURKEY

TURKMENISTAN

TAJIKISTAN

NORTH
KOREA

JAPAN

PACIFIC
OCEAN

CANARY
ISLANDS
(Spain)

MOROCCO

TUNISIA

LEBANON

SYRIA

AZERBAIJAN

AFGHANISTAN

CHINA

SOUTH
KOREA

IRAN
IRAQ

KUWAIT

PAKISTAN

Tropic of Cancer

WESTERN
SAHARA
(Morocco)

ALGERIA

LIBYA

ISRAEL
EGYPT

JORDAN

BAHRAIN
QATAR

BHUTAN

NEPAL

BANGLADESH

TAIWAN

CAPE
VERDE

MAURITANIA

SAUDI
ARABIA

UNITED
ARAB
EMIRATES

INDIA

MYANMAR
(BURMA)

LAOS

NORTHERN
MARIANA ISLANDS
(United States)

WAKE
ISLAND
(United States)

SENEGAL

MALI

NIGER

CHAD

SUDAN

ERITREA

YEMEN

OMAN

THAILAND

VIETNAM

GUAM
(United States)

MARSHALL
ISLANDS

GAMB.
GUINEA
GUINEA-
BISSAU

BURKINA
FASO

BENIN

AFRICA

DJIBOUTI

PHILIPPINES

GHANA

NIGERIA

CENTRAL
AFRICAN
REP.

ETHIOPIA

SRI
LANKA

CAMBODIA
BRUNEI
MALAYSIA

PALAU

FEDERATED STATES
OF MICRONESIA

SIERRA
LEONE

LIBERIA

CÔTE
D'IVOIRE

TOGO

CAMEROON

SOMALIA

MALDIVES

Equator

KIRIBATI

SAO TOME AND
PRINCIPE

EQUATORIAL
GUINEA

GABON

CONGO

RWANDA

UGANDA

DEM. REP.
OF THE
CONGO

BURUNDI

KENYA

NAURU

TANZANIA

INDONESIA

EAST
TIMOR

PAPUA
NEW
GUINEA

SOLOMON
ISLANDS

ATLANTIC
OCEAN

ANGOLA

ZAMBIA

MALAWI

SEYCHELLES

COMOROS

INDIAN
OCEAN

TUVALU

NAMIBIA

ZIMBABWE

BOTSWANA

MADAGASCAR

MAURITIUS

VANUATU

FIJI
ISLANDS

N

W   E

S

SOUTH
AFRICA

SWAZILAND

LESOTHO

MOZAMBIQUE

RÉUNION
(France)

Tropic of Capricorn

AUSTRALIA

AUSTRALIA

NEW
CALEDONIA
(France)

SOUTH GEORGIA &
SOUTH SANDWICH
ISLANDS (U.K.)

FRENCH SOUTHERN &
ANTARCTIC LANDS
(France)

NEW
ZEALAND

Antarctic Circle

ANTARCTICA

EUROPE

NORWAY

SWEDEN

FINLAND

RUSSIA

North
Sea

DENMARK

ESTONIA

LATVIA

IRELAND

UNITED
KINGDOM

NETH.

Baltic Sea

RUSSIA

LITHUANIA

BELARUS

0   400 mi
0   400 km

ATLANTIC
OCEAN

BELG.
LUX.

GERMANY

POLAND

UKRAINE

FRANCE

LIECH.

CZECH
REPUBLIC

SLOVAKIA

SWITZ.

AUSTRIA

HUNGARY

MOLDOVA

SLOVENIA

ROMANIA

MONACO

SAN MARINO

CROATIA

BOS. &
HERZ.

SERBIA

GEORGIA

ANDORRA

ITALY

MONT.

MACEDONIA

BULGARIA

Black Sea

PORTUGAL

SPAIN

ALBANIA

TURKEY

GREECE

GIBRALTAR (U.K.)

MALTA

SYRIA

MOROCCO

ALGERIA

TUNISIA

CYPRUS

LEBANON

Mediterranean Sea

Glossary

avian influenza (AY-vee-en in-floo-EN-zuh) a potentially deadly viral disease found in birds that can also infect humans

Buddhist monks (BOO-dizt MUHNGKS) holy men of the Buddhist religion

cancer (KAN-sur) a disease marked by growths or tumors that can be deadly

contagious (kuhn-TAY-juhss) easily transmitted from one person to another through contact; usually used to describe a disease

diabetes (dye-uh-BEE-tuhss) a disease in which the body produces little or no insulin, a substance that allows the body to break down and use sugar in food; it can be treated but still leads to many deaths

influenza (in-floo-EN-zuh) a viral infection that is often contagious, or easily passed from one person to another

mutate (MYOOT-ate) to change

passport (PASS-port) a document that identifies a person's country of origin and is used to cross national borders

pedicabs (PED-ee-cabz) three-wheeled vehicles with seats, driven by a person pedaling as if on a bicycle; they are used for transportation in some countries, especially in Southeast Asia

SARS (SARZ) Severe Acute Respiratory Syndrome, a highly contagious type of pneumonia

Spanish Influenza (SPAN-ish in-floo-EN-zuh) a viral respiratory infection that is highly contagious; it killed millions of people between 1918 and 1919 in one of history's most terrible pandemics

summit (SUHM-it) a meeting of high-level leaders from different nations that addresses an international concern

vaccines (VAK-seenz) medicines that help prevent diseases by strengthening the body's ability to fight them

virulent (VIR-uh-luhnt) able to spread quickly and cause much harm

For More Information

Books

Grady, Denise. *Deadly Invaders: Virus Outbreaks around the World from Marburg Fever to Avian Flu.* Boston: Kingfisher, 2006.

Miller, Debra A. *Pandemics.* San Diego, CA: Lucent Books, 2006.

Peters, Stephanie True. *The 1918 Influenza Pandemic.* New York: Benchmark Books, 2005.

Web Sites

Centers for Disease Control and Prevention: BAM! Body and Mind
www.bam.gov/sub_diseases/index.html
Learn more about how scientists track diseases and how you can prevent them

Kids' Health—Bird Flu
www.kidshealth.org/parent/general/sick/avian_flu.html
Learn about the symptoms and preventive measures for the avian flu

Science News for Kids—Fighting Off Micro-Invaders
www.sciencenewsforkids.org/articles/20031105/Feature1.asp
Read an article about fighting off epidemics like SARS

WHO—Epidemic and Pandemic Alert and Response
www.who.int/csr/en
Learn about the preventive measures the World Health Organization takes when faced with a threat such as SARS or the avian flu

INDEX

ABOUT THE AUTHOR

Robert Green has written more than 30 books for students. He is a regular contributor to publications on East Asia by the Economist Intelligence Unit and holds graduate degrees from New York University and Harvard University. He witnessed the outbreak of SARS in Taiwan in 2003 and was required to wear a mask to work there during the outbreak.